The Baby Boomer's Guide to Retirement, Health and Happiness

The Baby Boomer's Action Plan to Financial Security and Longevity

Robert Edwards

This book is dedicated to my beautiful wife who I love and adore more with each passing day.

Copyright Act of 1976, the scanning, uploading and electronic sharing of any part of this book without the explicit written consent or permission of the publisher constitutes unlawful piracy and the theft of intellectual property.

If you would like to use material or content from this book (other than for review purposes), prior written permission must be obtained from the publisher.

You can contact the publishing company at admin@speedypublishing.com. Thank you for not infringing on the author's rights.

Speedy Publishing LLC (c) 2014
40 E. Main St., #1156
Newark, DE 19711
www.speedypublishing.co

Ordering Information:
Quantity sales; Special discounts are available on quantity purchases by corporations, associations, and others. For details, contact the "Special Sales Department" at the address above.

This is a reprint book.

Manufactured in the United States of America

TABLE OF CONTENTS

PUBLISHER'S NOTES i

CHAPTER 1: INTRODUCTION 1

CHAPTER 2: THE TIME TO TAKE CHARGE IS NOW 3

CHAPTER 3: THE TRUTH ABOUT AGING 8

CHAPTER 4: BABY BOOMER'S NEED TO ADDRESS THEIR DIET 13

CHAPTER 5: WHY BABY BOOMER'S NEED TO EXERCISE 19

CHAPTER 6: HORMONES AND SUPPLEMENTS 29

CHAPTER 7: THE IMPORTANCE OF THE BABY BOOMER'S BRAIN .. 37

CHAPTER 8: FINANCES 41

CHAPTER 9: IMPLEMENTING LIFESTYLE CHANGES 46

CHAPTER 10: The To Do List 51

MEET THE AUTHOR 53

Publisher's Notes

Disclaimer

This publication is intended to provide helpful and informative material. It is not intended to diagnose, treat, cure, or prevent any health problem or condition, nor is intended to replace the advice of a physician. No action should be taken solely on the contents of this book. Always consult your physician or qualified health-care professional on any matters regarding your health and before adopting any suggestions in this book or drawing inferences from it.

The author and publisher specifically disclaim all responsibility for any liability, loss or risk, personal or otherwise, which is incurred as a consequence, directly or indirectly, from the use or application of any contents of this book.

Any and all product names referenced within this book are the trademarks of their respective owners. None of these owners have sponsored, authorized, endorsed, or approved this book.

Always read all information provided by the manufacturers' product labels before using their products. The author and publisher are not responsible for claims made by manufacturers.

Chapter 1: Introduction

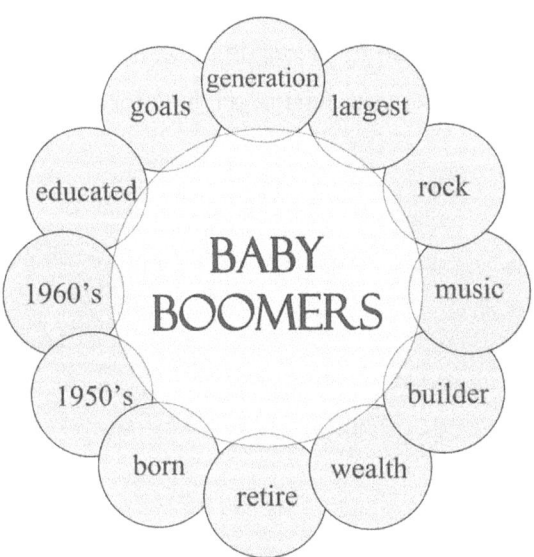

Are you a baby boomer? If you were born in the years between 1946 and 1964 then technically you are considered a baby boomer. But, even if you fall out of this range, this book is a tool that you must take into consideration today.

Those that are approaching late middle age and into their golden years need to begin thinking about their futures. While it would be wonderful to be able to just stop the clock, that's not possible. What is possible is finding the things that can help you to improve your well-being, your health and ultimately to lead you to a long, healthy and prosperous life.

If you haven't given any thought to your future, now is the time to do so. There are countless things that need to be thought about, but, it's all in here, ready to give you the tools you need to really make a difference.

Read this book. Take the time to make these changes in your life today. And, set a course for a long life that is full of the riches that the world can offer to you. Best of all, look forward to many years of bliss.

Chapter 2: The Time To Take Charge Is Now

Time is fleeting. It just doesn't last as long as we would like it to last. Although it may seem like just yesterday you were raising your children, those years have passed and now they are raising their own children. But, before you let any more time slip pass, start thinking of your future.

Although you may not be able to go back and adjust time, implementing the changes in your diet, your exercise, your mental health and in your financial health will allow you to find the necessary tools to excelling in your later years. If one thing is for sure it is that you can make a difference in the quality of the rest of your days if you take charge now, without wasting any more time.

Why Didn't You Do It Before?

Although you may be kicking yourself for not saving enough money or for not dropping those extra 40 pounds when you were younger, hold fast in the thought that you can still make progress by making changes today. In many ways, you'll be able to find the health and wellness that you could have had.

If you are younger, there are many changes that you can make today that will greatly impact your life later. In fact, if you simply make a few of these changes today, you'll be able to far exceed your goals in earning a savings account that can pay for retirement, in fending off heart disease and even keeping Alzheimer's at bay.

Every day that you implement positive change, is one more day that you have the ability to gain benefits. The sooner you start the more benefit you can obtain.

Why Should You Make Changes Anyway?

One of the largest in importance and probably the most difficult things to change is your mind.

Why can't I just live the way that I want to today?

Why can't I just eat the foods that taste good and live the life that I am living?

What's going to happen if I do this for one more day, month or year?

You may not realize it, but each of these things can and will lead you to a premature death. Living one more day eating foods that are unhealthy will lead to the increased risk of heart disease. Living one more day with not getting enough sleep, not relieving stress and not getting the exercise you need, leads to disease and an immune system that can't keep up with you.

Living one more day, takes off more time at the end. Is that really what you want?

There is good news, though. Most of the damage that you've done to your body can be reverse if you have done so in time and are dedicated to making that happen. With just a few minutes of care to your lifestyle each day, you can get back the time you may have possibly lost. Don't think that it has to be forever, because if you can change your mind, you can get it back.

What's To Change?

You don't have to live a life that's super "clean" and yes, you can make mistakes, eat that fatty hamburger and still watch realty television if it makes you happy. But, the goal that should be realized is that these things should be done in moderation.

There are many things that you should take into consideration as being things to change. Here are a few of the most important considerations that you may have to make changes in.

1. **Your Diet:** Giving your body the nutrients it needs is vitally important to living as long as possible. Not only do you need to put good things in, but you need to get the bad things out.

Giving your body the tools it needs to make this happen is important to living longer.

2. **Your Brain:** Stimulation to the brain needs to be on going. With the population's number of Alzheimer's cases expected to drastically increase with the Baby Boomer generation, it is virtually important that you provide the tools necessary to curb this if possible.

3. **Your Finances:** It is expected that in the next five years, more than 50 percent of those that enter retirement will not be able to support themselves but will rely on family, Social Security as well as charity. Is your financial future set for retirement?

4. **Your Physical Fitness:** It is critical that your body be physically fit. That means that the 2/3rds of the population in the United States that is overweight or obese needs to take heed. Heading into your later years with this type of physical problem will definitely shorten your life span.

5. **Your Lifestyle:** Getting social interaction, being happy, and less stressed are all key ingredients to a healthy and happy lifestyle. If you don't incorporate these types of interactions into your life, you lose mental alertness and your quality of life is just not what is should be.

Each of these five things can be changed in simple ways and in large ways to help you to prepare for the later years of your life. In fact, no matter where you are in your life, developing your own future is something you have the ability to change. That doesn't last forever, though.

Giving yourself an opportunity to excel is something you must do and you need to begin making the changes now. The good news is that we've broken it all down for you into a simple guide that will transform your life for the future.

In the next chapters of this e-book, we'll talk about these five elements and give you step by step methods to changing your life to improve the future.

Take the time to fully read through these pages, but then go back and begin implementing them into your life today, when it counts. If you wait, you waste your future.

Now, let's start building a quality life.

Chapter 3: The Truth About Aging

Walk into any department store and you'll find hundreds of beauty products lining the shelves. Each one of those products has something else, something unique to offer. Most promise to hide the signs of aging. Some make claims of being able to erase the years and to have you looking 10, 20 or more years younger. But, in truth, there is no way to avoid aging, is there?

Consider some numbers for a moment.

In the late 1800's and early 1900's, the average life expectancy in the United States was that of just 42 years of age! Today, that number has nearly doubled its size and that's no short feet to accomplish. The fact is that people are living longer because of the benefits of modern medicine and the benefits that technology offer.

In fact, today, there are over 70,000 people in the United States alone that are at the age of 100 or more! That is an outstanding number.

As you watch your parent's age, you are probably thinking to yourself the things that you would have done different, so that you don't walk down their same path.

Perhaps you would like to be more active so that arthritis doesn't set in so soon. Or, perhaps you would be tested sooner than they were for cancers, heart disease and countless other conditions. The good news is that you do have the ability to see these things going wrong and therefore you should be able to reach out and lengthen your lifespan.

One way we like to think that we can do this is by looking younger. That's why all of those products are on the market. If it wasn't a multi-billion dollar business, there wouldn't be so many products trying to take part of that chunk of change. But, what type of anti-aging product can you possibly invest in that's going to improve the quality of your life?

What if we told you that it really had nothing to do with those products on the market, but that it had to do with the things that you are capable of making changes with today, right now?

That's what this book is all about. But, before you get to those good tidbits, it's important for you to understand that you don't just want to look younger. You need to dig deeper into your lifestyle and feel younger.

With modern medicine and modern science, we have a much better understanding of how the things around use affect us. We know that cancer can be caused by toxins entering into your body when you breathe and we know that some forms of heart disease happen because of the foods we eat. But, we also know how virtually everything else on planet earth affects us too.

By taking that knowledge and using it to look for ways to improve our aging faculties, you are able to truly transform your life to a point that goes beyond that of what any of those anti-aging wrinkle creams can do.

Research Has Guided Us

Research by skilled doctors has guided us to these answers. For example, some researched are so dedicated to anti-aging that they've developed a protocol that will lead you through the process. For example, take a look at these signs of aging.

By the time that you are 35 years old, the amount of hormone that your body makes has sharply declined. The stress you are under, the foods that you eat and the city's air quality has led to little particles getting into your body (these are called free radicals, by the way!) They get into your cells and can be the beginnings of cancer. Even though you feel good, the process has already started.

Or, by the next stage, by the time that you are 45, even more destruction has happened to the body, especially the individual cells in your body. Hormones have further dropped and now, your body is starting to show signs of aging. Your skin, your hair, and even your energy levels are showing signs of aging.

At this point, if you are still getting high levels of free radicals entering your body, it is at the point of leading to the development of cancer, if it hasn't already.

Still, it gets a bit worse when you move past this age. Now, things are completely working against you. Lower hormones, again, and your skin is drier. It has thinned considerably because your body has stopped making enough collagen to support it. Your joints are chiming in now with the first aches and pains of arthritis. Your energy levels have fallen considerably.

If you fall victim to heart conditions, diabetes, or hypertension, your organs have started to fail you. Of course, heart disease is likely to be the type of disease to kill you.

Yes, it does sound grim. But, because researchers do have this wealth of an understanding about your body, they can now help you to make changes that will improve your health and help you to gain freedom from much of this.

What is important is to address the body not as a whole but as individual cells, by which it is composed. By taking into consideration the vast number of cells and their needs, you can provide the appropriate attention to the conditions that face them, improve your health and wellness and eventually help yourself to live a longer, healthier life.

While you may want to consider dieting and exercise as the best ways to stay healthy, even this is not the right path to follow. What you should be doing, then, is creating a plan that specifically treats your body in the hopes of working as an anti-aging tool.

The next chapters are dedicated to the fundamentals of this plan. By doing these things they will help you, the Baby Boomer, to live longer and healthier. Remember, being developed by researchers that have one goal in mind, anti-aging, helps you to know that these things are going to help improve your life today and well into the rest of your life time, no matter how long that is.

CHAPTER 4: BABY BOOMER'S NEED TO ADDRESS THEIR DIET

Here's an exercise for you.

What did you eat this morning or today, for that matter? Did you eat a well-balanced diet that's full of whole grains, lean proteins, vegetables and fruits?

Or, was your breakfast a cup of coffee and maybe a bagel, loaded with cream cheese of course?

You are what you eat. The Standard American Diet is a term that's been coined to describe the fast food crazy, greasy, fatty and high sugared diet that most Americans eat. Even if you live on the other side of the planet, chances are good that you aren't eating a diet that's rich in the foods that are important to your aging process.

In fact, the foods that you are eating that fall into that type of diet are what are playing the largest single part in killing you prematurely. As a Baby Boomer, you have plenty of life still left in you and your diet is the perfect place to begin making some serious changes. Just look at what it is doing to you!

If you have a larger midsection to your body, then you have a high risk of having a heart attack due to heart disease. Just a few extra pounds are all it takes.

If you consume a diet that is rich in salt, you are destroying your kidneys as well as some of the other organs in your body.

If you are eating fatty foods, you're killing you heart by suffocating it under layers of cholesterol.

What Diet Should I Follow?

If all of this scares you, which it should, you may be considering a diet. Yes, a diet does sound like a good idea but the problem with them is that it is ultimately impossible to stay on that diet for your lifetime. That leads to the potential for you not to follow it for long, allowing virtually none of the important benefits to come through to you. That's not what you want.

Diets that go from one extreme to the next are everywhere you look. Those that facing a diet that is high in protein are still putting their heart's at risk because of the increase cholesterol there. Those that are following a low fat diet are doing the opposite. They are not giving the body enough protein to build muscle mass, which actually helps you to burn fat faster.

Because diets are so extreme, they rarely work for people that are facing these conditions.

But, you don't have to face these problems to be able to gain the benefits that you need. In fact, the most basic of diets is one of the best ones to follow for your health and well-being.

Enter The Baby Boomer's Perfect Diet

Now, instead of thinking of this as a diet, think of it as a better way to eat. It is not something you'll ever come off of and it is not something that you should throw to the side. It is a way of life and although there are some things you will have to give up, it is still one of the easiest diets to follow.

In fact, if you do decide to eat something that you shouldn't, if you just go back to eating well from there out, you'll still be okay. It is all about controlling how much of the bad stuff you take in and making sure that the good stuff is what comes in more often than anything else.

Here's what you should be doing. Split up the foods that you eat into a pie graph. 50 percent of what you eat should be good carbohydrates. The next 25 percent of the foods you eat should be lean proteins. The final 25 percent should go to fats.

This way of eating is enjoyable and it's easy to follow. Here are some more specific points that you should install into your eating plan.

1. The carbohydrates that you consume should be made up of mostly fruits and vegetables.

2. The proteins that you eat should be from beans, tofu and other types of plant sources. About 1/3 of the protein you eat should come from animal meat and then it must be lean.
3. For fats, you want to obtain this from good fats such as olive oils and nuts instead of fats that come from animals. Look for poly and mono saturated fats for this section.

That's it. You pick the foods and as long as they fit within this diet regimen, you know you are working on creating a healthy and anti-aging diet that will propel you to health and wellness.

When to Eat Matters

It should be mentioned that you shouldn't sit down to a large meal, either. Instead, you should be eating four, five or even six smaller meals per day.

One of the most important things that you need to "get over" when it comes to the food part of your life is that food doesn't have to be the center of attention. You need to disconnect the feeling of needing food to make you feel comfortable and relaxed. Learning this will be a requirement because you need to detach from the mentality of sitting down to a large meal.

If you have problems going from eating four to six small meals per day, try to add a fruit into your middle periods. This can help to stabilize your blood sugars to help you to feel better.

Getting Sugar Out

One of the key methods to improving your life for the future is to look at sugars. Refined sugar should be avoided at all costs. Why is sugar so bad for you? When you consume sugars, you are increasing the body's production of a substance that is called cortisol. That is a hormone that actually speeds up the aging process and can lead you to aging faster.

Now, to remove junk food from your body, you should start with the sweets. You don't want to excessively eat foods like junk food. You also want to cut out the soda that you drink as that too can add refined sugar to your diet that you simply shouldn't have.

If you are craving something that is sweet, look towards healthy, whole fruits. Low sugar is good, but no sugar foods are even better for you.

Your Ideal Baby Boomer Weight

One thing that is a major difference from most other diets and weight loss plans is that with the Baby Boomer's Diet, you need to install a diet that allows you to drop weight. You should be looking to weigh about five to ten percent less than what you have been told your ideal weight is. That's not to say that you should starve yourself, but dropping these extra pounds will encourage a great deal of benefit in your body.

Here's a method to figuring this out that can help be a guide for you.

Women: The weight that you want to follow should be 100 pounds for your first five feet of height. Then, add on five pounds for every inch taller that you are.

Men: The weight that you want to follow should be 106 pounds for the first five feet that you are high and then an additional six pounds for every inch after that point of height.

Are you worried that you can't follow this type of diet? Do you think that it may be too restrictive of you? Remember that although this lifestyle is something that you should follow, that doesn't mean that it should be strictly followed without one falter.

If it's your birthday, sure you want a piece of cake. Having a small piece of cake won't hurt you if you go back to your healthy Baby Boomer diet afterwards. If you have a sweet tooth, satisfy that sweet tooth with a piece of fruit instead of candy.

As we mentioned, there is no aspect of your life that is more important than improving your body's physical condition. As you will see in the next chapter, it is important to incorporate a healthy exercise regimen as well. This coupled with a healthy diet will deliver for you the optimal health and wellness for years to come.

It is essential for you to make these diet changes so that your body doesn't take in the wrong things. You will see that if you adjust your diet to this type of plan that you will begin to feel good quickly.

Chapter 5: Why Baby Boomer's Need To Exercise

Everyone hates the word exercise, but it is a vitally important component to health and well-being. With so many people striving for improved health, there are gyms opening up everywhere. On top of this, you'll find countless opportunities to do simple exercise at home.

But, when we are talking about the health and wellness of the Baby Boomer, there is much more to it than just this. In fact, it is essential that you install a plan of overall exercise that incorporates several key types of exercise and movement.

Why Does Exercise Have To Matter?

Since we were children, we were encouraged to get outside and play. Today, the children that aren't doing this are unhealthy and overweight. Many have problems with learning and attention deficit problems. Much of this can be blamed on the fact that they don't get out there and play.

As a Baby Boomer, it's important for you to realize that exercise can do many things for your health and well-being. In fact exercise, when done correctly, will actually help you to look and feel younger.

Yes, this could be considered the anti-aging tool of a century because it can be that powerful when done correctly.

Have you ever been the type of person that did exercise regularly? If you ever went through a phase of going to the gym and working out, then you know that exercising does make you feel good. It makes you healthier too.

- You are stronger and therefore can accomplish more for longer periods of time.
- Your muscles are lean and fit, which means that they are less prone to injury or pain.
- Your body is working at optimal levels which help to keep the immune system working well.
- Your heart is working hard and therefore becoming stronger with each workout that you do.
- You are likely the right weight which means that you have less chance of heart attacks.

There are many ways that exercising makes a difference in the body and the Baby Boomer cannot ignore these facts if he or she is going to improve their overall health and well-being.

Now, what do you need to do to gain the benefits that exercise can offer to you?

There are actually three key parts of the exercise regimen that you want to install into your life as part of your regular program. This is not a program that should be done only for a certain time period but over the course of your lifetime as long as your doctor approves of it.

By incorporating these key elements into your lifestyle, you will actually be building a healthier body that will live a longer and healthier life.

The three things that you must take into consideration include these:

- Your Heart: You need cardiovascular training that is centered on improving your heart's function.
- Your Muscles: Strength training is necessary for you. You need to improve the function of your muscles.
- Your Joints: Flexibility training increases the range of motion and discourages the onset of conditions such as arthritis.

If you don't believe that it's important to take into consideration any of these elements, consider these very frightening facts:

When you turn 60, you can look forward to having lost at least half of the strength you used to have. You also won't be able to count on not breaking a bone if you fall because your bones are much weaker. In addition, your lungs can't pump out nearly the amount of air as they used to.

But, if take the time to install an exercise regimen like the one we are encouraging you can completely wipe away these risks and improve your health and well-being considerably.

How to Do It

First and foremost you should see your doctor before starting any type of exercise regimen. This will insure that your body is healthy enough to handle what you are going to do to it. Don't worry; you won't be hurting yourself unless you don't take this first step.

Once you get the all clear from your doctor, you can begin at looking for solutions to your exercise needs. First, start by working on your heart.

Improving Heart Function

To do this, you'll want to take into consideration the aerobic exercises. If you get in an aerobic exercise program, you will help improve your heart considerably. During these workouts, you are pushing your heart to its limits. As you do that, you are also encouraging it to strengthen. Aerobic exercise improves your heart's function.

How much aerobics do you need to get in? For most people, it is necessary to do an aerobic exercise at least three times a week for at least 20 minutes per day. That's only one hour of your time that you are dedicating to aerobic exercise and you will see improvement.

But, for that improvement to happen, you do need to pay attention to what you are doing. In order to see benefits, you need to get your heart pumping at the right speed. To measure this, you will want to increase your exercise intensity to a level that is no more than 65 percent of your maximum heart rate.

To determine what that is, do this. Start with 220 and take away your age. Then, multiply that number by .65 (you can go as high as .75 if you are physically fit.) You want to get your heart rate to that level for at least 20 minutes three times per week.

Check out the web for ways to learn how to measure your heart rate. Or, a better solution is to ask your doctor about what your maximum heart rate target should be. When doing this level, it should be difficult to talk but not so bad that you feel exhausted.

Strength Training

While aerobic training is important, so is that of strength training. Don't worry; you don't have to work out so that you have bulging muscles. But, you do need to have some exercise regimen that incorporates building your muscle mass.

Strength training is actually the use of weights and movements that will increase the size and function of the muscles in your body. Although some individuals only think of strength training as weight training, the two are completely different. You don't want to over develop your muscle groups, but you do want to increase them in the way of health.

Increasing your muscle mass is important for a number of reasons. The key element will be to help you to maintain a healthy weight. You see, lean muscle mass, which is the type of muscle that you develop through strength training, is actually better at burning through stored fat. It also is helpful at burning calories faster. The combination means that they can help you to get rid of stored fat that you have throughout your body.

In technical terms, when you add additional muscle mass to your body, it is able to be more metabolically active than that of the fat that is stored in your body.

By increasing your muscle mass, you increase your metabolism as well. That means that your body remains lean and trim, which is ideal for heart health as well as overall organ health.

But, what if you don't have weight to lose? Even when you do drop to your ideal weight or if you are already there, it is still quite important for you to take care of this aspect for other health reasons.

Lean muscle mass is important for optimum health. Your body, especially your muscles, are trim and they can then pump blood easier. In addition, they are less likely to be injured or to develop problems later in life. The longer that your muscle groups are healthy, the longer that the rest of your body does well.

If you end up being in a sedentary lifestyle because of injuries and just lack of energy (something else that is a benefit from strength training) you can end up with countless health conditions that go along with it.

In addition to all of this, strength training also aids in keeping the heart strong. With the right training, you can increase the pumping power of the heart.

How much strength training you do depends on your needs for weight loss and your current muscle condition. One of the best things to do to gain both this type of exercise as well as aerobic is to join a gym or visit your local recreation center where you can work out weekly.

Again, with strength training like that of aerobic training, a regimen of three times per week is ideal for weight benefit and muscle training benefits.

Keeping each of these functions of your body healthy is something that you absolutely need to do. But, even with aerobic training as well as strength training, there is more that you'll need to tackle to complete the entire exercise package.

Flexibility Training

Believe it or not, you have to do your stretching. Stretching is yet another key function of improving your health and well-being. One of the key reasons that you need to use flexibility training is that of keeping your joints healthy.

Did you know that the onset of arthritis can start any time after the age of 25 (even younger sometimes)?

The arthritis that you feel now is only going to get worse and since it is a degenerative disease, it is likely to leave you with deformed, disabled joints. But, with the help of flexibility training now, you can avoid these conditions all together.

Flexibility training keeps you moving right. By stretching, you help your muscles to stretch and therefore keep them from getting hurt. Your muscles become lithe and limber. You can move like you did when you were in your 20's, accomplishing the things that you want and need to do. When you increase your body's ability to move in all directions, you feel younger and your body is actually improving in age, too.

Stretching and toning your muscles and joints is an important part of improving your overall health. With this type of training, you can keep your joints working optimally and you reduce your risk of strains, pulls and sprains significantly.

One of the most common complaints today from the Baby Boomer age is that of back pain. No matter what you may have done to it or what you think is wrong with it, back pain is a very common condition that happens more and more as you age.

But, when you add in a strength training workout to your exercise regimen, you improve the quality of those muscles and increase your spinal's movement and flexibility. You actually reduce the pain that you may be in and even prevent further injuries from happening to your back or hips, yet another common pain location for the Baby Boomers today.

A flexibility training regimen should be done at least 3 times per week for 20 minutes at a time. If you want to see rapid improvement here, you should try to do some form of stretching each morning and each evening. Just a few minutes of doing this will increase your body's tone and flexibility and it's a great way to start and end the day!

Pulling It All Together

Now, does all of that sound like it is just too much to do? It doesn't have to be.

In fact, really all you need is just 1 hour three times per week. Or, you can break apart these workouts to give yourself less of a lump of time commitment. You need:

- 20 minutes of aerobic training for heart health three times per week.
- 20 minutes of strength training for muscle improvement three times per week.
- 20 minutes of flexibility training for movement and joint improvement, three times per week.

A great way to gain these benefits is to invest in a membership to a gym. To help you to get started, work with a personal trainer, telling them what your goals are. You don't have to continue working with them but after a month or so of training, you'll be able to do your workout routine on your own. Just don't falter from it or you'll have to start all over again.

For flexibility training, consider taking in a yoga class or another type of easy movement training. This too is something that you can learn and then do on your own if you would like to.

When you do these things, you get to transform your life in so many ways. Consider the people that you know that are over the age of 60. When you meet John and he shakes your hand, do you feel how weak and frail it is? Do you feel his bones and realize that this once very large and tough man is now frail and very weak. You may even feel like you could break his hand if you hold onto it too hard.

Is that the type of handshake that you want to give? Or, do you want to be able to firmly grasp someone's hand and feel the strength coming through? When you incorporate an exercise regimen like this, you can gain those benefits and so much more.

In addition to this, exercise can actually help to improve your age. Aerobic training as well as strength training helps to stimulate your body to produce growth hormone. This hormone is a key ingredient to improving the health of your individual cells. If you remember, improving each of your cells is important in keeping yourself healthy longer.

Therefore, when your body produces more growth hormone, it can actually reverse the aging that your body has already gone through. That's because growth hormone actually can restore the health and the youth of each of your cells.

One important thing to realize from this is that through exercising, you can improve much if not all of the damage that you've done to your body over the years. You can restore your youth to a degree and then maintain it for some time to come.

Exercise simply must be a part of your life. The Baby Boomer requires this type of movement for benefits that come later on in life, too.

Chapter 6: Hormones and Supplements

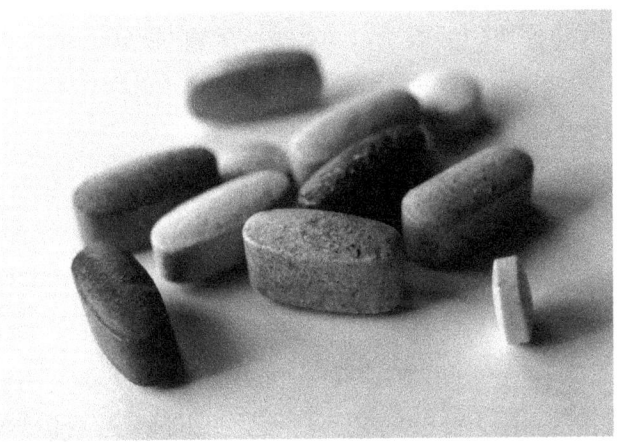

As a combination of the diet and exercise regimens of the Baby Boomer, it is also important to take into consideration supplementation and your body's hormones, both of which are critical at preserving the body's health and longevity.

You may ask why you need to add supplements to your diet when you have just started on a healthy diet that's been described here. The reason for this is really unfortunate for most.

Even with a healthy diet that is filled with just the nutrients from healthy food, you are still not getting all of the nutrients that you need to maintain optimal health. This is due to several key things including the way that your food is grown. For example, the way that your food is farmed has allowed for the soil to be depleted for many of the nutrients that you need. Many of these nutrients can actually help you to improve the longevity of your life.

Supplementation is needed for other reasons as well. Here are some examples of why you need to add the right nutrients to your diet now.

- Pesticides and herbicides are commonly used to help keep bugs off of the foods that are grown. While you think that this is a good thing, it still causes problems for the production of nutrients in the soil.
- The soil itself is often not even authentic soil! Some of the most modern farms are using synthetic types of soil which allow for faster and longer growing seasons that produce more products that's also good looking.
- With genetic mutation, scientists of have developed fruits and vegetables (not to mention virtually any other type of food that you eat) products that are genetically altered enough to produce the perfect specimen every time. The nutrients get left out.

As you can see, there are many reasons that the foods you eat don't have the nutrients that are needed to increase the longevity and health of your life. Still, you should also realize that even when you do get the right foods, you still have so many other factors that play a role in the way your body uses them. The sugars that you eat, the fats, and the high amounts of sodium cause the real nutrients to get lost in the mix. Your body doesn't get a chance to bring them in.

When you don't get the right types and amounts of nutrients, your body will break down faster with the onset of degenerative diseases. In fact, some studies have shown that with the proper nutrients you can die early. As you know, we are working on keeping you healthy, longer and supplementation can take us there.

What Do You Need In Supplements?

As we mentioned, it is quite important to insure that you are eating a healthy diet, like the Baby Boomer diet that we've described. But, in addition to that, supplementing your diet with the right vitamins and minerals will also be important.

Here are some things to remember about supplements in regards to what you should be consuming.

Select supplements that are right for your body. This should take into consideration your age, sex and your current health situation. Remember, you need to insure that the supplements you take will help improve the rate at which you are aging.

Antioxidants are an important part of the supplement that you take. Find one that offers a high amount of antioxidants which help to remove free radicals from your body. They help to deter diseases like heart disease and cancer. In addition, they help each of your organs to work better. Antioxidants also help to stimulate natural growth hormones to be released throughout your body.

You also want the supplement that you select to provide you with the necessary nutrients to help keep your organs running at the highest level. You want a product that will keep problems like heart disease at bay as well as Alzheimer's disease.

Mood benefiting products are also important. You want a product that will help to relieve stress and improving your general state of well-being.

The supplement that you take should also promote a healthy sex drive in both men and women. Not only is that something that you will want to have working optimally, but it also helps to secrete hormones that are necessary for health in the long term.

Look for a supplement that provides cellular rejuvenation. This means that the product will help in the restructure and repair of the cells of your body. You want the supplement to be able to promote this well-being in each of the cells of your body.

Your hair, nails and skin should also be aided by the supplement hat you take. You want a product that will promote healthy skin cells and healthy, young looking nails and skin.

You should also look for the supplement to be a time released product as these generally are able to enter the body slowly and therefore are absorbed better into the body. Other products that are water soluble simply get washed away.

Finally, take the time to find out what's in the supplement. You want to find a supplement that is as natural in composition as possible. You should check to see if it has the Food and Drug Administration's seal of approval, but that is not always available.

Take the time you need to compare the products that are on the market. Instead of trying to find many supplements, each offering its own unique benefit, look for a supplement that features many of those that you need. A good place to start is to take your list of needs to your local nutritionist or to the health food store (you can shop for them online, too, of course!) Have them help you to find the perfect supplement for your anti-aging, health promotion.

Finally, when you get to the point of saying, "why am I doing this, again?" Consider this.

In the standard American diet, it would be necessary for you to consume a 5000 calorie diet in order to get the nutrients that you need for optimum health and even then some of them would be left out! Since the recommended diet is that of just 2000 calories (on the high side) you can see how this would be counterproductive to your efforts. Supplementation then, is a must.

A combination of healthy products is what you need to look for. That means vitamins and minerals but also herbal products. You'll find that the more natural the product is, the more benefits it can provide to your overall health and well-being.

Hormone Soup

The hormones that your body releases are very important to your well-being. As a Baby Boomer, you are likely already facing the depletion of the most important hormone in your body: growth hormone.

Growth hormone is important for a number of reasons. For one, it helps your body to grow and develop. But, it also helps to rejuvenate and repair the damage to your cells. In many ways, this growth hormone is responsible for the decline in your body over the years. It is, in short, what makes you look aged.

Now, if you could increase the amount of growth hormone in your body, you could potentially slow the aging process. In fact, those people that have the ability to live a life that has been riddled with all of the "bad stuff" and still somehow live to be 100 are tell-tale signs of this.

You see, in most people, the growth hormone that is so important to our longevity begins to taper off at the age of just 25! Each decade of your life, it will decrease yet another ten to fifteen percent leaving you with next to nothing. But, those that do live to see 100 are often a part of a small group of people that have a gene that keeps the growth hormone working optimally in their body for long after the point when most turn off, so to speak.

But, just because you don't have the ability to alter your genes doesn't mean that you can't help to keep growth hormone production happening in your body. No, we don't mean through artificial supplementation or any type of injections. You can do this through natural and non-side effect riddled ways.

If you did try to use an artificial type of supplementation of growth hormone, you would have to visit your doctor to get it. In addition, the wrong about can actually cause very severe side effects, including the possibility of death. Therefore, this is not the best way to get the growth hormone that is necessary for longevity.

You can, on the other hand, encourage your own glands to continue producing it. By stimulating the pituitary gland, you can actually allow it to begin providing your body with the necessary release of this hormone again. The type of product that you would use to make this happen is called secretagogues. These are all natural products which mean that they are generally safe to use, with few to no side effects.

Taking these supplements will help to provide you with some amazing benefits. You'll see improvements in your skin and in your hair first. You may even begin to have a sex drive again. By increasing your body's excretions of other hormones such as DHEA, progesterone and testosterone, it can also help improve the health and well-being of many aspects of your life.

Since your body requires hormones to help make things happen in your body, getting them to be balanced and secreted as they can be a wonderful thing for the rest of your body. For example, just increasing the right hormones in women after menopause can delay or even avoid osteoporosis, heart disease and even help to fend off cancers and other health concerns that you may have.

As you can see, with the help of secretagogues, you can find the benefits of health and well-being that you are seeking. To find these products, you can talk to your local health store or you can look for them available on the web. Whatever you do, don't forget to include them in your diet and exercise regimen.

As you can see, the need for supplementation and for hormone stimulation is vitally important when it comes to maintaining your health for a longer period of time.

Although you may often be told that the things you do are what drive your age and how long you'll be healthy. But, there are factors that you can't control such as the growth hormone and the foods that you eat not having enough of the nutrients your body needs.

But, you can also see how you can repair these elements by simply including supplements into your diet. You'll also find that it is easy to tackle these problems once you have the right products to take.

Yes, supplements may seem like a nuisance when you have to take them daily. But, adding a pill a day, so to speak, can really help to keep your organs working correction, keep your skin from looking aged and it can give you the nutrients you need to live a long and happy life. You definitely want that!

Chapter 7: The Importance of The Baby Boomer's Brain

Your brain is one of the most important things for you to take into consideration in any health regimen. For the Baby Boomer, it is even more vitally important to care for your brain.

Today, the number of Alzheimer's patients is quickly on the rise. There are numerous situations in which people are forced to realize that the years are slipping by and they no longer can keep a grasp on time.

There is no doubt that over time your brain is going decrease in function. You are going to lose some of its function over time. But, when that happens is what you should be worrying about.

With the right tools and planning, you can delay significantly these reductions. In some cases, you can even minimize the extent to which they happen to you. The good news is that the things that you can do to keep the mind stimulated and functioning correctly are things that are easy to do and even can be enjoyable.

There are a number of things you can do, actually, each of them offering their own benefit. Here are some.

Learning

Learning is one of the very best things you can do to your brain. As you age, many stop doing new things and looking for new areas of the world to explore. That is what starts the shut-down of the brain. Because you aren't using it as much, especially for new things, you aren't making it function as much as it needs to.

When you keep your brain functioning, you encourage it to continue to be active. On the other hand, if you don't, you lose the necessary functions that you need.

Some ideas here include taking a new class, learning to do something that you enjoy such as a new hobby, and even learning history. You can take courses at your local community college or start a discussion group about the books that you are reading. Learn to plan a new instrument. Learn to cook like a professional.

Stay Socially Active

Another thing that you need to do to help keep your brain healthy is to stay in the social scene. Involving yourself with others and keeping yourself part of the group helps your brain to function well beyond what it normally would.

If you become someone that lives alone, talks to no one and simply does the same things day in and day out, there is little hope that your brain will stay stimulated. But, encouraging your brain through relationship building, stimulation from others and just being with other people can help to keep your own brain active.

In addition, most people love to be around others and that in it-self can be a blessing to the brain. Doing things that you love improves your overall well-being.

Stay Physically Active

We've talked a lot about the need for physical activity but it is also important for your brain as well as the rest of your body. Because physical exercise stimulates circulation in your body, you'll actually be adding the circulation of blood to the brain. What's more is that if your body is physically active, your mind will be more likely to be physically active as well.

Doing the exercise regimens that are included here will help the Baby Boomer in body as well as in mind.

Brain Food

The nutrients that are required for your health and well-being are also important for your brain. It is essential that your body gets the right amount of nutrients for brain stimulation and health. One of the most important elements in that are Omega 3 fatty acids. These can be found heavily in fish or you can take them in supplemental form.

These nutrients are essential for the health of your brain. When you are developing the right supplement for your Baby Boomer body, it should include supplements for your Baby Boomer brain, too.

Keeping your brain active is very important to your overall well-being. Without taking in these considerations, you put your brain at risk for becoming ill and functioning less optimally. As you can see, though, this is one of the most prosperous and easy parts of the Baby Boomer's lifestyle that can be changed for the better!

Chapter 8: Finances

One of the largest worries that a baby boomer has to deal with is the financial aspect of life. It may seem strange to include the money aspect of your life in this book, but the Baby Boomer needs to take into account the financial obstacles that they are beginning to experience.

Many baby boomers are already seeing the financial crunch as they watch their parents struggle to pay the bills. Some of them are seeing that their parent's homes are being reversed mortgaged to pay them something back so that they can actually afford daily life. Even worse, should they need long term health care and end of life care, they aren't sure of just how that's going to be paid for.

But, there is a problem. The Baby Boomer generation is also the generation that changed the world with their care free attitude.

They started their lives in a post war period that was quite prosperous, didn't have to worry about saving because many of the years have been economically beneficial to them. And, now, most baby boomers don't have the funds that will allow them to retire.

Baby boomers liked to spend, and they spent more than any other generation before them. They also liked to mortgage real estate, run up credit cards and even have started more businesses than any other generation.

What does all of this mean to you, though?

As a Baby Boomer, is it incredibly important for you to invest the time and money into looking at your financial situation.

The first thing you need to address is how long you'll be working. Many Baby Boomers plan to work longer. Since this generation has aged well to this point, they are expected to live longer. But, that doesn't mean that they will be leaving their jobs at the standard age of 65 which is what Social Security allows them to do.

Instead, many of them, more than half, will continue to work longer. Some will retire only to work part time, start their own business or work without pay. The smallest percentage of Baby Boomers plans to never work again after they retire.

The question is, what can you financially do?

Many of your parents didn't spend their time determining just how expensive it will be to afford health care and even more so the cost of living that is today. For that reason, many more are living off of Social Security, help from family and even elderly care services.

But, you don't have to find yourself in this position. Here are some tips that can help you to get your finances in order so that you can work or not work at your leisure when you reach your retirement.

- Savings: The largest component of being able to live well after you retire is the money that you have in the bank. Of course, if you haven't started saving at this point, you still should be considering it. The payments that will come in from Social Security are likely to be quite low in comparison to the lifestyles that most Baby Boomers live today.
- Spending: Many Baby Boomers like to spend. But, now is the time to reel that in some so that you can afford to spend longer into your future.
- Determine what pension, 401k or other type of investment you have and manage it. It will be incredibly important for you to learn how these funds are doing. As you approach retirement, you'll need to readjust the funds to be more conservative so that you don't lose it all.
- Invest wisely: Although there is plenty of time to invest and see a nice return, it is also something that should mean more risk to you now. You'll want to do the research needed and work on your risk tolerance to determine the best opportunity for you.

The Key to Success

Since each financial outlook is different from one Baby Boomer to the next, one of the most beneficial tasks that you can take on is to find a financial advisor. While we have talked a lot about the things that you can do to improve your life's longevity, you need someone that can financially make that possible. A skilled financial advisor will provide you with the knowledge to make the right decisions, ultimately.

They can help you to determine how to spend, invest and save your funds. They can help to develop a strategy that will allow you to fund the lifestyle that you are living today well into the future. Working with you, they will help you to find out what things you can do differently now, so that the financial reward comes later.

What You Need To Plan For

What you may not realize is just what you need to plan for. With the longevity that you'll get from being healthy, you will need funds that will take you through your entire life. If you have a lifestyle that you are comfortable with right now, you'll want to maintain that in the coming years as well. With financial advice, that can happen.

In addition to this, more and more people are looking at traveling, exploring the world and enjoying the luxuries that life has to offer. With this also comes an added cost. While these things are excellent tools to keep your mind stimulated and your body healthy, you'll need to be able to afford them.

In addition, there is health care to consider. With the rising costs of just stepping foot into a doctor's office, it is becoming increasingly important to find a way to afford this too. The risk of counting on insurance companies or government funded medical care is quite limiting and can often place you where you don't want to be.

Even still, many Baby Boomers still have homes to pay off that are mortgaged at least one time. This means that you'll need to be able to make enough to use this money wisely. While there are options like reverse mortgages that allow you to be paid a sum of your home's value each month, this comes at a high price and may not be the right decision for your needs.

Beyond anything else, the Baby Boomer generation is one that likes to set life at their own pace and likes to do things their own way. Having changed the world, you may just need some extra funds to make that continue, too.

If you are a Baby Boomer, it is time now to make the decisions regarding your finances for the future. If you don't make these critical decisions now, then the funds won't be there when you need them.

Invest your time and money into a solid, trusted financial advisor that you can work one on one with. Learn what they can offer to you and find out just what it is that you can expect from them. With the dedication of these individuals, you will quickly find your place in the financial lifestyle you want to live.

The Baby Boomer must address money concerns now, while they are healthy and while they have the time to make changes. To live a prosperous life, you need to manage the financial aspect of it as well as the health aspects.

Yet, this doesn't have to be difficult with the right people by your side to make it happen.

Chapter 9: Implementing Lifestyle Changes

One of the most difficult things for the Baby Boomer to change is that of his lifestyle. That's why we've left it until now. You knew it was coming. You have to give up drinking, smoking and all of those other things that are ripping apart your health and well-being. We don't have to tell you those things, but if you don't do them, nothing you've learned here is going to prolong your life any more than they will shorten it.

But, lifestyle changes don't have to be for the bad. There are actually many small things that you can do to improve the overall quality and health of your life without having to give up the things you love.

On the other hand, there are those things that you do have to take into consideration and repair. You do have to set your priorities straight and you do have to make sure that your health becomes the most important thing in the world to you. That's no short order.

And, we'll start with the hardest yet most important one of all.

Stress

Baby Boomers are known for the stress that they are under on a constant basis. Challenge is something that many of you live for. In fact, more than 40 percent of the Baby Boomer generation will continue to work not for the money but for the mental stimulation and challenge that it provides to them.

Nevertheless, stress can be detrimental to your overall well-being. In fact, it will shorten your life span if you don't do something about it right now.

Why does stress play such an important role in your life? There are a number of reasons why, but when it comes to what stress does to your body physically, the evidence is in.

Stress is known as the silent killer because it affects virtually every part of your body. Not only does it cause trauma to your brain, but it will cause muscles and joints to become injured, organs to not work as well and allows your body to remain open to illness.

In addition, it helps you to age faster. Because stress increases the amount of cortisol that your body produces, you age faster. Cortisol is an element that actually increases the speed at which you age. The longer and more severe the stress is, the more damage it does to you.

The good news is that most of the damage that comes from stress can be repaired and even elevated. But, this does mean that you need to make some lifestyle changes now to make that happen for you.

For starters, stressful situations like work environments that are negative or cause you to remain in a state of stress are not good for you and should be changed. Although you may not believe that you can do this, the stress you face there will shorten your lifespan and worsen your health in the short and long term.

Here are some ways that you can reduce stress even when you can't leave the job behind.

- Physical activity will help to reduce stress. Going for a walk, playing a sport, and even the exercise that you get in your Baby Boomer exercise regimen will all help you. By pumping oxygen rich blood throughout your stressed muscles, you improve the overall function of them and therefore help your body to relax.
- Mental relaxation can also help. Learn how to do yoga (remember it's great for stretching too!) or you can learn to meditate. You can also find other quiet activities that can help to relax you.
- Take on a new learning experience. Learn how to do karate, meet new people and expand your knowledge base through reading. Finding these things to do will encourage your brain to work more successfully and it will encourage stress relief.
- Do things that you enjoy. Getting a massage will help to melt away stress. Go for a walk or go swimming. Spend time with family and friends just playing a game. These small things make a considerable difference in stress reduction.

But, stress isn't all that you need to take into consideration when it comes to lifestyle changes.

Those Habits

As mentioned, those habits that are bad for you, such as smoking, drinking alcohol and illegal substances should not be done. The sooner that you stop doing so, the better it can be. The good news is that some of the damage from smoking will repair itself on its own. But, alcohol damage won't be so lucky.

Even if you need a cigarette to relax, the bottom line is that smoking and drinking will lead to cancers of the lungs, brain cell deterioration and much more. The circulatory system alone suffers greatly at these risks.

There are many helpful groups available today, that your doctor can help you to find that can help you to make these changes so that they aren't too hard to do or too taxing on your daily life.

Positive Attitude

Be happy. In short, improving your mood and giving yourself more opportunities to be positive can also help to increase your longevity and help you to remain healthy, longer. Although doctors don't fully understand why, many patients that that face life threatening conditions that have a positive attitude going in are the ones that actually pull through. Even in the worst of situations, having this full of life, positive mental attitude can pull you through when even medicine can fail.

To stay positive, you should do things that you enjoy. Since most Baby Boomers are still working, that means cutting back those hours a bit and enjoying a picnic in the park, relaxing after dinner and just enjoying the peace of the afternoon. Catch a nap, call and talk to a friend for an hour about nothing and even spend the day laughing and carrying on.

Doing things that you enjoy doing is beneficial to your overall health. As we mentioned earlier, it helps to stimulate the brain. But, it also helps to improve your quality of life. Let's face it, nothing that you learned here can be beneficial to you if your quality of life is minimized in any way.

Getting through the difficult times is hard to do and still stay positive. Some find the hope and help they need in religion, while others seek out answers in science. Even still, many just look at the benefits and blessings they have now and hope they continue for a long time in coming.

Doing whatever it takes to improve your lifestyle will ultimately lead you to a lifestyle that is positive and overall beneficial to your goal of a long, prosperous lifestyle.

CHAPTER 10: The To Do List

Now that you have the necessary information, get moving on implementing each one of the changes that we've covered here. Here's a checklist to help you to find those rewards now.

- Improve your diet today. Develop an eating plan that helps to promote longevity and health. Detach from eating for emotional support. Reaffirm your connection with a long life instead.
- Start to move. The exercise regimen that includes strength training, aerobic exercise and flexibility training will improve virtually any health condition you may be in.
- Improve your brain power. Include stimulating activities into your life daily to encourage your brain to keep growing and expanding instead of shutting down.

- Take the time to consider supplementation and hormone changes that can ultimately encourage your body to live longer, healthier as well as to look amazing while you do it.
- Get your finances in order.
- Improve your lifestyle by cutting out the bad including the silent killer that stress is.

Meet the Author

Robert Edwards was in his forty's when he realized that his parents were financially struggling in their golden age of retirement. Health issues and medical bills compounded the issue and it was clear that his parents were going to outlive their nest egg.

With his wife's blessing Robert was able to financially assist his parents, but what if he hadn't been in that position? This reality check put Robert into motion. He immediately took action on planning for his financial security and re-evaluated his health habits.

Cuts in the household budget and the family's lifestyle were made to pay off debt and invest as much as possible for retirement. The outcome was worth it and allowed Robert to retire comfortably earlier than originally planned.

Retirement planning starts today no matter how old you are or what your economic situation is. It is never too early or too late to plan ahead. Putting it off another day or another year only hurts you and your loved ones.

Robert is sadly aware that many baby boomers may be economically forced to work well into their 70's or until their health fails them. Robert wrote this book to help anyone who is willing to read it and consider their financial future and the importance of good health.

In retirement Robert enjoys playing golf, restoring classic cars, brewing beer, spending time with his family and traveling with his wife.

www.ingramcontent.com/pod-product-compliance
Ingram Content Group UK Ltd.
Pitfield, Milton Keynes, MK11 3LW, UK
UKHW022120230426
12048UKWH00010BA/622